KU-068-002

PROPERTY OF

2 4 JAN 2008

CAMDEAN PRIMARY

# Popcorn Pop

Practising long vowel phonemes,
CVCC and CCVC plus polysyllabic words

First published in 2007 by
Franklin Watts
338 Euston Road
London
NW1 3BH

Franklin Watts Australia
Level 17/207 Kent Street
Sydney
NSW 2000

Text © Sue Graves 2007
Illustration © Fabiano Fiorin 2007

The rights of Sue Graves to be identified as the author
and Fabiano Fiorin as the illustrator of this Work have
been asserted in accordance with the Copyright, Designs
and Patents Act, 1988.

All rights reserved. No part of this publication may be
reproduced, stored in a retrieval system, or transmitted
in any form or by any means, electronic, mechanical,
photocopy, recording or otherwise, without the prior
written permission of the copyright owner.

A CIP catalogue record for this book is available
from the British Library.

ISBN: 978 0 7496 7280 5 (hbk)
ISBN: 978 0 7496 7319 2 (pbk)

**Series Editor:** Jackie Hamley
**Series Advisors:** Dr Barrie Wade, Dr Hilary Minns
**Series Designer:** Peter Scoulding


Printed in China

Franklin Watts is a division of
Hachette Children's Books.

PHONICS

# Popcorn Pop

by
## Sue Graves

Illustrated by
## Fabiano Fiorin

# W
# FRANKLIN WATTS
### LONDON•SYDNEY

## Sue Graves
"Have you ever cooked popcorn? It's lots of fun ... and delicious to eat while it's still warm!"

## Fabiano Fiorin
"While illustrating this book I had such a craving for popcorn that I went straight out and bought some. I ate the whole box!"

Mum had to go to town. Paul was sad. "Pop will play with you," Mum said.

"Shall we make popcorn?" said
Pop. "I make very good popcorn.
I'm Popcorn Pop I am!"

"Cool!" said Paul.

Pop got out the popcorn.

Paul got out a plate.

11

"Now the popcorn must cook," said Pop.

13

"Shall we play football outside?" said Paul.

"Yes," said Pop. "But we must *not* forget the popcorn."

Pop and Paul had a lot of fun.
They soon forgot about
the popcorn.

"Oh dear!" said Paul, suddenly.
"I can hear popping!"

18

19

Pop ran inside.

There was a lot of noise.

20

Pop! POP! went the popcorn.

21

Pop got lost in a cloud
of popcorn.

Paul began to laugh and laugh.

"Look at this mess!" said Pop.

"We must clean it all up!"

Paul got the broom.

27

Just then, Mum came back.
"How kind of you to clean
for me!" she said.

"Look! I got
you this
in town!"

29

30

31

# Notes for parents and teachers

READING CORNER PHONICS has been structured to provide maximum support for children learning to read through synthetic phonics. The stories are designed for independent reading but may also be used by adults for sharing with young children.

The teaching of early reading through synthetic phonics focuses on the 44 sounds in the English language, and how these sounds correspond to their written form in the 26 letters of the alphabet. Carefully controlled vocabulary makes these books accessible for children at different stages of phonics teaching, progressing from simple CVC (consonant-vowel-consonant) words such as "top" (t-o-p) to trisyllabic words such as "messenger" (mess-en-ger). READING CORNER PHONICS allows children to read words in context, and also provides visual clues and repetition to further support their reading. These books will help develop the all important confidence in the new reader, and encourage a love of reading that will last a lifetime!

If you are reading this book with a child, here are a few tips:

**1.** Talk about the story before you start reading. Look at the cover and the title. What might the story be about? Why might the child like it?

**2.** Encourage the child to reread the story, and to retell the story in their own words, using the illustrations to remind them what has happened.

**3.** Discuss the story and see if the child can relate it to their own experience, or perhaps compare it to another story they know.

**4.** Give praise! Small mistakes need not always be corrected. If a child is stuck on a word, ask them to try and sound it out and then blend it together again, or model this yourself. For example "wish" w-i-sh "wish".

READING CORNER PHONICS covers two grades of synthetic phonics teaching, with three levels at each grade. Each level has a certain number of words per story, indicated by the number of bars on the spine of the book:

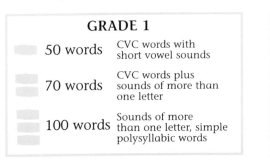

### GRADE 1

50 words — CVC words with short vowel sounds

70 words — CVC words plus sounds of more than one letter

100 words — Sounds of more than one letter, simple polysyllabic words

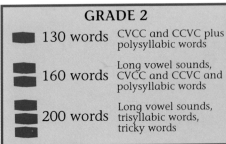

### GRADE 2

130 words — CVCC and CCVC plus polysyllabic words

160 words — Long vowel sounds, CVCC and CCVC and polysyllabic words

200 words — Long vowel sounds, trisyllabic words, tricky words